Los Lunas Dec

The Decalogue Stone.

Los Lunas Decalogue Stone

An Eighth-Century Hebrew Monument in New
Mexico

DONALD N. PANTHER-YATES

Panther's Lodge

Phoenix

CONTENTS

LIST OF FIGURES

To Father S.

Without Whose Help and Devotion

This Story Might Never Have Been Told

Then the Lord replied to Job out of the tempest and said:
Who is this who darkens counsel,
Speaking without knowledge?
Where were you when I laid the earth's foundations?
Have you surveyed the expanses of the earth?
-- Job 38:1-2, 18

1 Jews and Indians

THE Decalogue Stone outside Los Lunas, New Mexico, is a sight seen by few people. Its very location is something of a state secret. You need a twenty-five-dollar access permit from the public land office to go to it, only officials are very clear. They cannot, and will not, give you directions. I would never have found this Phoenician Hebrew version of the Ten Commandments had it not been for a local *chueta* (crypto-Jewish parish priest). In an age when Muslim and Jewish monuments worldwide are being desecrated, his name will remain as closely guarded as the stone's whereabouts. Suffice it to say that the Decalogue Stone rests in a hidden cleft amid the dry, juniper-studded hills south of Albuquerque, near the edge of the Isleta Pueblo Indian Reservation.

It was Professor Robert Pfeiffer of Harvard University who first translated the Decalogue Stone, in 1949. He identified it as a short version of the Ten Commandments as given in Exodus 20 and noted that the style of Hebrew letters on it was in use from about 1000 B.C.E. This dating would place it in the age of Solomon, builder of the First Temple in Jerusalem. It became the main focus of the

Epigraphic Society's meeting in 1984, after a full account appeared by Professor Joseph Navey of the Hebrew University of Jerusalem and his team.[1] Barry Fell reported later on the punctuation in the inscription.[2] Theories have continued to spring up about how an archaic Hebrew text of the Ten Commandments could have been incised in expert, ancient capitals in the face of a multi-ton boulder of volcanic basalt, one of the hardest minerals on earth. They range from a mad professor's joke, to a marooned Phoenician, to a troop of boy scouts, to you-name-it. Few seemed to want to believe it can exist, but there it was before my very eyes (Fig. 1).

It says, "*I am Jehovah thy God who hath taken thee out of the land of Egypt, from the house of slaves. There must be no other gods before my face. Thou must not make any idol. Thou must not take the name of Jehovah in vain. Remember the Sabbath day and keep it holy. Honor thy father and thy mother so that thy days may be long in the land that Jehovah thy God has given to thee. Thou must not murder. Thou must not commit adultery. Thou must not steal. Thou must not give a false witness against thy neighbor. Thou must not desire the wife of thy neighbor nor anything that is his.*

The inscription is marked with an unusual tree growing from beneath the boulder. This has serrated pea-green curled opposite pinnate leaves, twisted smooth gray

---

[1] ESOP vol. 10, part 1 (1982).

[2] ESOP vol. 13 (1985), pp. 35-41.

roots and stem, and a weeping ungainly shape, closest in my opinion to a honey locust. My source could tell me little about it except it was unique, with beautiful golden foliage in autumn. After doing some research, I believe it a rare False Acacia (R. *Pseud-Acacia tortuosa*). Since the prized garden plant was first introduced into North America in 1640, this *terminus ante quem non* seemed to lend credence to the explanation that it was Spanish crypto-Jews who carved the stone it shades. Perhaps I should have said "guards." Several species of acacias contain cyanide and can cause sudden death. Others are the source of gum Arabic and medicinal balms.

Ever since the Spanish set foot on New Mexican soil in 1590, the Land of Enchantment has been a "Promised Land" for Jews. An estimated forty percent of the colonists immigrating from Spain to the New World were noted in records to be of Sephardic Jewish ancestry. In the nineteenth century, New Mexico became a haven for German Jews. Unfortunately, this whole chapter in the history of the Southwest has been handled in a step-motherly fashion. There is no single comprehensive source book on its crypto-Jews, only scattered treatments. Most of the information about Jews in New Mexico has been disseminated through radio programs and newspaper accounts. Stanley Hordes, who stumbled onto the secret of crypto-Jews when he was appointed New Mexico State Historian, wrote a dissertation on them and later published a timid monograph on the subject.[3] A bolder and better book is Richard G. Santos, *Silent Heritage. The Sephardim and the Colonization of the Spanish North American Frontier 1492-1600* (New Sepharad Press). Furthermore, a good overview of the state's Jewish experience can be found in Henry Tobias's *A History of the Jews in New Mexico* (University of New Mexico Press). Yet few of the publications pursue the thread of crypto-Judaism back beyond the mid-seventeenth century. For the whole story we are dependent on rare witnesses willing to talk, like our *chueta*. On his father's side he is descended from *genizaro* Manuel De La Mora from Belen, while his mother's matrilineal line goes back to a Pueblo Indian woman. Moreover, as proven by DNA he is a Sephardic Cohen, traditionally claimed to descend from Aaron, the brother of Moses. So, like Tony Hillerman's heroine in *Skinwalkers*, the priest's ancestry is Jewish and Native American.[4]

---

[3] Stanley Hordes, *The Crypto-Jewish Community of New Spain, 1620-1649: A Collective Biography*, Ph.D. Dissertation, Tulane University, New Orleans, 1980. In December 2001, the *Atlantic Monthly* magazine published a hostile attack, "Mistaken Identity? The Case of New Mexico's Hidden Jews," by Debbie Nathan and Barbara Ferry.

[4] Santa Fe DNA Project, available online at http://www. familytreedna.com/public/NuevoMexico/. The Cohen Modal Haplotype was studied by Michael F. Hammer, Karl Skorecki, and their colleagues in a January 2, 1997 paper in *Nature*, volume 385, entitled "Y Chromosomes of Jewish Priests." This launched an

It seems Jewish Indians are an old joke. The Austrian writer Else Lasker-Schüler styled herself an American Indian, and Franz Kafka died proclaiming he wished he had been a "Red Indian." The metaphor reaches back to a Yiddish playlet, *Tsvishn Indianer*, an 1895 entertainment translated as "Among the Indians, or the Country Peddler." Fanny Brice's claim to fame was the song "I'm an Indian," and comedians Eddie Cantor, Woody Allen and Mel Brooks milked the same gag.[5] Today, Marx Toys makes an accessorized series of "Cherokee Chief Black Hair The Movable Indian," described as looking "very much like the actor Ed Ames (Mingo of Daniel Boone show)," the Jewish-American entertainer (who is of Russian Askenazi parentage).

---

entire industry of commercial DNA fingerprinting. See also Karl Skorecki, David Goldstein, et al. in *Nature*, volume 394, "Origins of Old Testament Priests," as well as the fascinating proof that the Lemba tribe of South Africa carried the same Jewish DNA in *American Journal of Human Genetics*, volume 66. The priestly sect Cohanim (singular Cohen) were all members of the Tribe of Levi. Aaron was anointed as the first High Priest (Cohen Gadol). From DNA analyses, it appears that New Mexico's Sephardic Cohanim are closer to the original Palestinian type than their Ashkenazic cousins.

[5] See Lilian Friedberg, "Dare to Compare: Americanizing the Holocaust," *American Indian Quarterly* 24/3 (2000) 353-380.

Fig. 1. Decalogue Stone and its guardian acacia tree.

My own family tradition handed down that one of my ancestors was both an Indian chief and member of a *minyan* in Daniel Boone's Kentucky. Were there any securely documented Jewish Indian chiefs? I immediately googled,

14

"Who is the most famous Jewish Indian?" The answer: Norman Greenbaum, Sixties musician and creator of the one-hit wonder "Spirit in the Sky." That sent me on a rough-and-tumble sabbatical through the obscurities of crypto-Judaism, Indian mascots, the theory of the Indians' descent from the lost tribes of Israel, Freemasonry, the Spanish Inquisition, the Watauga Settlements in Tennessee, and the history of the Confederacy.

The American Jewish Historical Society had one candidate that answered the description. Don Solomono Bibo, Jewish Indian Chief, was born in Prussia in 1853. His brothers preceded him west, and they all settled in New Mexico in 1866. The Bibo brothers worked for the Spiegelberg family of pioneer merchants. Eventually they set up a trading post to exchange goods with the Navajos, and Solomon joined them from Germany at the age of sixteen, in 1869. He soon became governor of Acoma pueblo. In 1885, he married Juana Valle, the granddaughter of his predecessor, who converted to Judaism. Their children were sent to Hebrew school in San Francisco. "Solomon Bibo, governor of the Acomas, America's only known Jewish Indian chief, is buried with his Indian princess in the Jewish cemetery in Colma, California."

In November of 1999, the New Mexico Jewish Historical Society dedicated its 12th annual conference to "the Jewish pioneers of the Territory of New Mexico and the

Pueblo Indians with whom they became so close." The keynote speaker was Mel Marks, author of the 1995 book *Jews among the Indians.* A picture of Jake Gold, "among the first Jews to settle in Santa Fe, with unidentified Pueblo Indian woman and baby" decorated the program, and conference goers could view the first public display of Solomon Bibo's revolver.

I felt better about my heritage when I read about Indian Jews in an article on Crypto-Judaism on the Internet. Many Portuguese and Spanish Jews, despite the laws against Jews emigrating to the New World, fled to Latin America, hoping to escape the long arm of the Inquisition. Unfortunately, the Inquisition followed close behind. There were auto-da-fe's and arrests in Mexico City and Antioquia in Colombia well into the eighteenth century. The grisly machinery of the Holy Office was not shut down until the 1820s.

> Some of the "secret Jews" joined themselves to another persecuted group: the indigenous people who were the majority population at that time in Latin America, the "Indians." They intermarried with them, forming what is now called *"Mestizo Jews."* The most well-known group of *"Mestizo Jews"* is in Venta Prieta in eastern Mexico. They look like American Indians, but have "reconverted" openly to Judaism.

Unfortunately they have for the most part received much rejection by the ethnically "pure" Jews of Mexico City. A notable exception was Rabbi Samuel Leer [Lerer], a Conservative Rabbi who arrived in Mexico City in 1968, and became their spiritual advisor. He performs marriage ceremonies for them once they formally convert to Judaism, and helps their sons through the Bar Mitzvah process. He performs the conversions [he said], "not because they need to but in order not to antagonize the other rabbis here . . . ." Every couple married since 1968 as well as the children born to these couples are now incontestably Jewish.[6]

The big question was how long Jews had been among the Indians. From my own understanding, after talking with

---

[6] Rick Aharon Chaimberlin, "Crypto-Judaism in America," online article from *Petah Tikvah (Door of Hope)* 16/2, available online Nov. 17, 2001, at http://www.nashuanh.com/bmy/Crypto.htm (since removed). We confirmed this story with Rabbi Lerer personally when he gave the keynote address at the annual conference of the Society for Crypto-Judaic Studies in San Antonio, Texas, Aug. 3, 2003. Rabbi Lerer was ordained by Chief Rabbi Ha-Cohen Cook. He used to tell converts, "You are Jews, crypto-Jews, but now I'm going to open you up!" Even though many of these were returning to Judaism after a lapse of 500 years, Rabbi Lerer considered their conversion "symbolic." The congregation in Puebla, Mexico, was named Beth Smuel after him.

American Indian elders over the years, was: ever since there have been Jews.

American Indian cultural anthropology has gone through an exciting period in the past fifteen years. Beginning with Greenberg's 1987 work on language and extending through Cavalli-Sforza's *History and Geography of Human Genes*, many of our notions about this "one percent of the population that accounts for 50 percent of the country's diversity[7]" have been challenged and reformulated. In an article on human lymphocyte antigens, Guthrie sums up and significantly adds to the growing consensus about the peopling of the Americas. A tentative chronological outline lists no fewer than 28 discrete migration events from 40,000 B.C.E. onwards, all substantiated by medical research, gene typing, and anthropological literature.[8]

One unpleasant thorn in the flesh of dogmatic geneticists in the last decade has been Haplogroup X. This European mitochondrial gene type occurring in American Indian populations has a fascinating story. It was reported

---

[7] H. L. Hodgkinson, J.H. Outtz & A.M. Obarakpor (1990) *The Demographics of American Indians: One percent of the people: Fifty percent of the Diversity*. Report prepared for the Institute for Educational Leadership, Inc. and Center for Demographic Policy. Washington, D.C.: U.S. Government Printing Office.

[8] James L. Guthrie, "Human Lymphocyte Antigens: Apparent Afro-Asiatic, Southern Asian, and European HLAS in Indigenous American Populations," *Pre-Columbiana* 2/2-3 (2001) 90-163.

only seven years ago.[9] Its addition to the four orthodox Native American lineages inspired the hunt for more "minor" founding mothers. What was most controversial about it was the suggestion that it might be an ancient link between Europe and North America, representing a founding lineage that traveled across the Atlantic Ocean (as, for instance, Stanford proposed in 1997). Perhaps it explained the mysterious Red Earth People of ca. 5,000 B.C.E, presumed to be circumpolar. Simultaneously, the race was on to find X in Asia or prove it was the result of recent admixture. In the meantime, Kennewick Man was unearthed, an 8,000-plus-year-old skeleton declared to be Caucasoid, and recognized as resembling modern Europeans more than Native Americans. This intensified the debate on who are Native Americans, and how and when people first came to the Americas. The Kennewick skeleton has been in and out of court ever since.[10]

---

[9] Michael D. Brown et al (1998) "mtDNA Haplogroup X: An Ancient Link between Europe/Western Asia and North America?" *American Journal of Human Genetics* 63/6:1852-1861.

[10] See David Hurst Thomas, *Skull Wars: Kennewick Man, Archaeology, and the Battle for Native American Identity* (Basic, 2001).

19

2 *Introducing the Phoenicians*

"The facts pouring in from every side bring us to the...general conclusion that ancient American civilization was stimulated by transoceanic contacts from the east and west; among them contacts with the Mediterranean were especially creative. This is, for example, also borne out by the discovery of Alexander von Wuthenau-Hohenthurm that before 300 A.D. no American Indian types are depicted in the tens of thousands of sculptured ceramic figurines from Mesoamerica, but only Far Eastern, African Negro, and various Mediterranean types—especially Semites."[11] The author of this surprising verdict was Cyrus H. Gordon, and his words came in the aftermath of an archeological bombshell called the Metcalf Stone. Gordon was professor of

---

[11] Alexander Von Wuthenau was an art historian and Professor of Art at the University of the Americas in Mexico City. Although he argued that the ancient and early Americas were filled with an international mélange of peoples from Africa, Asia and Europe (*Unexpected Faces in Ancient America, 1975*), he specifically identified a group of carved heads as "Moorish-looking." Found in Mexico, such heads are dated between 300 - 900 C.E. and another group between 900 -1500 C.E. One such artifact of the former period von Wuthenau describes as "an old man with hat."

Semitic studies at Brandeis University and an expert on Hebrew, Phoenician, Aramaic, and Ugaritic. The Metcalf Stone was a small flat piece of sandstone turned up by a Georgia man hunting for suitable materials to construct a backyard barbecue pit in 1966. Most scholars today acknowledge that the writing on it is Minoan, executed by the same ancient mariners who built the palace at Knossos on Crete in the second millennium B.C.E. As Gordon wrote, "After studying the inscription, it was apparent to me that the affinities of the script were with the Aegean syllabary, whose two best known forms are Minoan Linear A, and Mycenaean Linear B. The double-axe in the lower left corner is of course reminiscent of Minoan civilization. The single vertical lines remind us of the vertical lines standing each for the numeral '1' in the Aegean syllabary; while the little circles stand for '100.' "

In 1994, epigrapher Gloria Farley published the results of nearly fifty years of fieldwork in and around her native state of Oklahoma. The massive book was titled *In Plain Sight;* a second volume was anticipated at the time of this writing (2005). "Evidence of Old World visitors to the coast of the Gulf of Mexico does seem to have been discovered," began Farley, quietly. In addition to the Metcalf Stone, she mentioned four other artifacts. We list them because they are all relevant to our story.

21

Fig. 2. These pre-Columbian painted marble statues, found along the Etowah River in Cartersville, Georgia, hardly correspond to one's mental image of ancient Native Americans. The bony, elongated oval faces, large noses, and thick lips point rather to a Semitic type. The female figure (right) is detailed with a cloth head covering, belt, and skirt. Both originally wore copper gorgets (removed by grave looters). *Etowah Indian Mounds State Historic Site.*

Much like the discoverer of the Metcalf Stone, Minna Arenowich was working in her flowerbed on Cedar Street in Columbus, Georgia, when she dug up a bronze Roman coin. It bore the image of Antoninus Pius (emperor 135-161 C.E.). In 1963, Mrs. Joe Hearn of LaGrange was also digging in her yard when she unearthed a small lead tablet with strange symbols. These were eventually identified as cuneiform, a script from ancient Sumer (modern Iraq) and dated from about 2040 B.C.E. "According to the translation, the scribe Enlila, who knew that it was the twenty-seventh or twenty-eighth year of the reign of Shulgi, listed a gift of sheep and goats to the sun-god Utu and the goddess Lamma-Lugal of Sumer" (p. 11). A coin found in Phenix City by a small boy in 1957 was "probably minted in the Carthaginian colony in Iberia." The boy took it to a local grocery store where he traded it for fifteen cents worth of candy. It can be compared with a bronze coin owned by the author recovered from the soil of South Carolina and dated to around 146 B.C.E., the year of the destruction of Carthage by the Romans (cf. p. 277, Fig. 3). The fourth object was a four-foot-tall stone standing on the banks of the Chattahoochee in Carroll County incised with an image initially dubbed "the Indian princess," but later identified as a Celtic goddess surrounded by North African Tifinag script (p. 10). It is now in the collection of the Institute for the Study of American Cultures (ISAC) at Columbus State University.

Archeologists often dismiss such finds because they did not come to light in the progress of an official excavation of a known site. Who is to say that someone did not plant the Roman coin in Minna Arenowich's garden? The same

Fig. 3. Carthaginian coin shows goddess Tanith on the obverse surrounded by dolphins (much crimped) and a horse and palm tree on the obverse, Punic emblems of state.

objection, however, cannot be raised with the Bat Creek Stone. It was exhumed in a tomb containing the skeletons of an East Tennessee chief and eight retainers by the Smithsonian's own William Emmert in 1889. Bat Creek is a tributary of the Little Tennessee River in the heart of Cherokee country about thirty miles southwest of Knoxville. Cyrus Thomas, head of the Smithsonian's mound survey, thought the epigraphy an example of historical-era Cherokee writing and published it in 1894--upside down.[12] The stone was then tossed in a back room of the Smithsonian and largely forgotten until Cyrus Gordon. He identified the letters inscribed on it as Paleo-Hebrew in square capitals diagnostic

---

12 "Mound Explorations," in *Twelfth Annual Report of the Bureau of Ethnology to the Secretary of the Smithsonian Insitution, 1890-91*(Washington: Government Printing Office, 1894), pp. 391-4.

of the second century C.E., reading (from right to left): יהוד
קר ל RQ L'YHWD, "a comet/*roq*/phoenix for Judea."[13] It is
now on indefinite loan from the National Museum of Natural
History to the McClung Museum of the University of
Tennessee (catalog number 134902; Fig. 4).

**Fig. 4. The Bat
Creek Inscription.**
*McClung Museum,
Knoxville.*

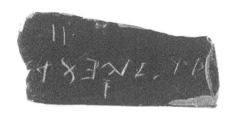

A firestorm broke out to prove Gordon wrong. In an
effort not lacking in elements of anti-Semitism, the forces of
academia were carefully marshaled to show that the Bat Creek
Stone was a fake. After several decades, skeptics seem to have
had the last word.

Or have they? The definitive exposé appearing in the
venerable journal *American Antiquity* in October of 2004 has
not been answered (Mainfort and Kwas). In one reply, still
under preparation, a professor at Ohio State University seems
to have successfully disposed of its arguments (McCulloch).
Rejecting comparison of the stone's Hebrew to a Masonic
treatise of 1870 – on which, more anon – McCulloch
reminded archeologists that a radiocarbon test performed on

---

[13] See Gordon 1971, pp. 136-7, Appendix.

wooden ear spool fragments found with the skull of the individual buried with the stone yielded a secure date "significantly pre-Norse, not to mention pre-Columbian . . . consistent with Gordon's first or second century A.D. paleographic dating of the text." He observed that the Bat Creek inscription contained peculiar letter forms and punctuation unknown to casual students of Hebrew in nineteenth century America, but evident in many other examples of ancient Square Paleo-Hebrew. "The fact that Cyrus Thomas, the Smithsonian's chief debunker of allegedly Old World inscriptions, did not see this glaring similarity, demonstrates, if nothing else, that he was incompetent for this task." Thus, the Bat Creek Stone appears to have been reinstated as a Jewish icon. Its authenticity has been confirmed.

The stone's reference to Jewish hero Bar Kokhba also appears to be vindicated, a connection first made by Gordon. *In situ*, it lay directly beneath the skull of the dignitary whose tomb the Smithsonian was excavating. "Comet for the Jews" was the slogan of a large-scale revolt against Rome 132-135 C.E., This last nationalistic insurgency of Israel before the Zionist movement of the twentieth century was led by Simon Bar Kokhba, whose name meant "Son of the Star."

Coins struck during Bar Kokhba's regime have been extracted in Kentucky – Louisville 1932, Clay City

1952, Hopkinsville 1967—and in southeastern Missouri from the St. Francis, a tributary of the Mississippi, 1922. . . . They read in Hebrew *Simeon* lower right around to lower left on the obverse and "Year Two [133 A.D.] of the Deliverance of Israel" on the reverse (Covey 1993 p. 76).

Thus, the connection with Bar Kokhba is supported by coin finds dating from the period of his rebellion (Thompson p. 179). And in 1860, a tablet inscribed in Hebrew with an archaic version of the Ten Commandments was found beneath a pile of stones near Newark, Ohio. Gordon elucidated this as a mezuzah (Jewish boundary or home marker).

How did Bar Kokhba and his men get to Tennessee? According to a continuator of Josephus, the ancient historian of the Jews, after their suppression "the Hebrews fled across the sea to a land unknown to them before." The country they settled in was Epeiros Occidentalis, the extreme limit of the West (Thompson p. 179). We also read that after the "devastating defeat of the Second Revolt under Bar Kokhba in 135, the Jews virtually abandoned Judea . . . . Others left for faraway places in the Diaspora where they knew Jews were living or welcome" (Biale p. 162, 165). Some rabbis had considered Bar Kokhba to be the Messiah (p. 164). Could the Bar Kokhba party have known they would be well received by the Cherokees, and is that why they went into exile where they did? Was there perhaps, as Melungeons later claimed, an Iberian Punic colony in North America?

Melungeons are a people who have been dwelling in the Appalachian Mountains of the southeastern United States for at least 400 years. The word could mean "cursed by God" in Arabic. Their origins have been the subject of intense speculation for at least three centuries, with theories ranging from shipwrecked Portuguese to ancient Carthaginians.[14] Typically, they are described as having dark skin, black or dark-brown straight hair, brown or blue eyes and European features. A popular culture book written by a self-identifying Melungeon (Kennedy 1997) renewed interest in investigation of the group's origins and stimulated an abundance of scholarly research. A detailed biogenetics study undertaken by Professor Elizabeth Hirschman of Rutgers University supported what Kennedy had earlier proposed: The Melungeons were, in part, a Sephardic Jewish and Moorish community that began as early as 1540 with the Soto

---

[14] Melungeons are sometimes also referred to as Black Dutch. The term Melungeon is also used in Brazilian history to refer to settlements by Portuguese Jews and Moorish adventurers among Amerindians of the Wild Coast: the great bulk of Brazil's African slaves came from Angola and were Malungin-speaking (a Southwest African language).

Expedition in what became the southeastern United States. The composition of this community grew over the intervening centuries with incoming Sephardic Jews and Moors who found refuge in such way stations as the Low Countries, Germany, France, Italy, Greece, and England after fleeing the Iberian Peninsula due to religious persecution.

Let us turn now from the Southeast to the Southwest to weigh additional evidence for Semites among the Indians. Bandelier National Monument lies twelve miles southeast of Los Alamos, birthplace of the atomic bomb, where Ph.D.s outnumber cowboys and Indians. When my wife and I moved from Georgia to New Mexico, we made a beeline to this famous Native American site. It is believed to be about a thousand years old. The road takes you through forests with elk herds and little sign of human habitation. Suddenly, you descend into a dry canyon with interesting huge cliffs of pockmarked tuff. We soon stood at the entrance to a shallow catacomb overhanging the exposed kiva and maze of interconnecting rooms of the stone and adobe village. There at its entrance was unmistakable proof that the ancient inhabitants had writing. Before us was a textbook case of Hinged Ogam (Fig. 7).

The general impression given by Bandelier is of a Greek or Roman or Tunisian site minus the temples and government buildings. The array of storerooms reminded me of Ephesus. I questioned one of the Park Service rangers

29

about the stonework. How did the people who lived here hew and dress all those blocks of sandstone, slate, and even granite? With obsidian knives, he explained. He pointed our party up the path to what he called Quetzalcoatl's Cave. According to anthropologists, Quetzalcoatl ("Feathered Serpent") was a mythic figure, a god associated with the wind and air, a prominent part of much Mesoamerican belief. We had no idea what a cave consecrated to him was doing in New Mexico, though one of us remembered that the English novelist D.H. Lawrence went on a bit about the Feathered Serpent when he lived in Taos.

However old it was, tens of thousands of dressed stones were required to build Bandelier, and hundreds, if not thousands, of metal tools. Obsidian shatters on stone. Nor can you use stone to chop stone: an archeological experiment attempting to do this produced an 80% degradation of tools within a few hours (Thompson 1994 p. 148). The first stone-cutting tools were discovered in the ancient Mediterranean world, and they were made out of copper. Lebanon was one of the first locations it was quarried, followed by the island of Cyprus, whose name means "place of copper." As veins were chiseled bare, its discoverers, the Phoenicians, moved on to Sicily, Sardinia, the Balearic Islands, and the Iberian peninsula. Zinc, a necessary alloy to create the strength of forged bronze, came from mines in Cornwall, along with tin. Bronze was the most coveted and essential material of its day.

As mines continued to be depleted, the pharaohs of Egypt dispatched Minoan, and then Phoenician, explorers across the seas to search for new sources. "They found one of the world's richest deposits in North America," according to one theory (Thompson 1994 p. 137). "Phoenicia's secret colonies were located along several major rivers, including the St. Lawrence, the Susquehanna, and the Amazon" (p. 146 – to which we can evidently add the Chattahoochee, emptying into the Gulf of Mexico, and the Rio Grande of New Mexico, also accessible from the same sea routes).

One of the world's richest copper deposits was located in the Lake Superior region of North America. Unlike the copper ores of the Middle East which required smelting, the deposits in Michigan and Ontario consisted of pure nuggets called 'native copper.' Some of the most accessible deposits were located on a large island called 'Isle Royale" in northwestern Lake Superior.... Minoan and Egyptian explores noticed [this] native copper when visiting tribes along the East Coast in 3000 B.C. . . . The New York Testing Laboratory has confirmed that [copper] artifacts found in American mounds were made using Old World casting technology. . . The shapes of the

31

copper tools found in American archeological sites are identical to those of the ancient Mediterranean, including chisels, dagger blades, wedges, hoes, scythes, axes and spear points . . . . After 1000 B.C. . . . since iron deposits were more plentiful than copper and did not require alloying to produce hardened metal, the demand for copper rapidly declined" (Thompson, pp. 146-149).

The age of iron had arrived. It, too, apparently reached into North America. Unlike copper, iron oxidizes and vanishes in the soil, but we have ample testimony to the fact that it was forged on this side of the Atlantic. Throughout the Ohio Valley, corresponding approximately to the distribution of Hopewell mound sites, are scattered thousands of ruined furnaces, foundries, and slag heaps. These were examined in 1951 by Arlington Mallery in a book titled *Rediscovery of Lost America*.[15]

Phoenicians were at the center of much of this activity. A Semitic people, they were originally Canaanite, like the Hebrews. They are probably the same as the Sea Peoples employed by the Egyptians to build such monuments as the Temple of Ramses III at Medinet-Habu. They became

---

[15] See also "America's Mysterious Furnaces," website at http://www.iwaynet.net/~wdc/.

important mercenaries on different sides in the turmoil that overtook the Nile empire. Allying themselves with the Lydians, they colonized Libya, and in 814 B.C.E founded Carthage as their capital. Throughout their long history, the Phoenicians mixed with many other nationalities, though they retained their Punic language and religion. The latter focused on the worship of Tanith, a sea goddess, and Bel (Baal), a male supreme being who demanded human and animal sacrifice. "For most of its history a closed society jealously guarding an Atlantic trade and colonial monopoly, Carthage remained an enigma to Greeks and to less curious Romans" (Covey 2004 p. 117). But it need not be a mystery to us.

It seemed we were getting closer to understanding why the Los Lunas Decalogue Stone was in Phoenician Hebrew.

3 The First Indians

CONSTANTINE Rafinesque was the Cyrus Gordon of his day. Living in a seminal period of American science, he made contributions to fields that were just then emerging. These included geology, stratigraphy, and archeology (Charles Lyell, *Principles of Geology*, 1830-1833), linguistics (Grimm's Law, 1819-1837), historical linguistics (Sanskritists A. W. and F. von Schlegel, and W. von Humboldt, founder of ethnolinguistics and linguistic psychology),[16] and bardic literature (Grimm, *Deutsche Sagen*, 1816-1818). Rafinesque developed a theory of evolution that predated Darwin by twenty years. He preceded the westward movement of Philadelphia intelligentsia in the "boatload of knowledge" that founded New Harmony in southern Indiana. It was

---

[16] "A direct line has been traced in American linguistics from Humboldt through D. G. Brinton (who translated some of his publications [and was Rafinesque's editor]), F. Boas, and E. Sapir to B.L. Whort, with particular reference to work on the languages of native America" (R. H. Robins, *A Short History of Linguistics*, Bloomington: Indiana University Press, 1974, p. 176).

Rafinesque who petitioned Congress to establish the Smithsonian (which it did, in 1846).

He was born October 22, 1783, to a family of Jewish merchants in the Ottoman Empire. Whether he is to be described as a Turk, Spanish-Portuguese Jew, Frenchman, or German is debatable, like much else about him. He was educated in Europe by private tutors, and he learned languages readily. From 1802 to 1805, he journeyed to America. Next, he opened an import/export business in Sicily, where he studied the natural history of plants and fish. Rafinesque returned to the United States in 1815 and three years later, he was appointed professor at Transylvania University in Lexington, Kentucky. Here he founded a botanical garden, one of the first in the New World.

Although the details are sketchy, it is here that he acquired the incised wooden sticks he published as the Walam Olum, purportedly the oldest specimen of Native American literature. Here also he wrote *Annals of Kentucky* (1824), a sweeping outline of American Indian tribal history.

Following his Kentucky years, Rafinesque moved back to Philadelphia, where he lectured at the Franklin Institute, continued to travel, and finished his career. Toward the end of his life, he suffered declining health caused by stomach cancer and his finances were destroyed. Altogether, Rafinesque authored more than 950 publications on natural history, philology, banking, economics, the Torah,[17] world civilization, and myth. He was also a skilled draftsman, surveyor, poet, and painter. But when he died on September 18, 1840, the much-moved contents of his rented quarters were sold at a hastily-arranged auction. His legacy was scattered.

Rafinesque's contact with local Native Americans and archeological sites in the Ohio valley led to his fusion of Old World learning with what might be called seer tradition, or American Indian history, in *Annals of Kentucky*. In it, Rafinesque narrated how the first "Indians" came from the Mediterranean:

> The Pelasgians[18] were bold navigators, and ventured to navigate from Iceland to the Azores and Senegal. The Azores, Madera, Canary and Capverd [Cape Verde] islands were then united in one or more islands, called the Atlantic Islands, which have given

---

[17] He published a book titled *Genius and Spirit of the Hebrew Bible* (Philadelphia: Printed for the Eleutherium of Knowledge and Central University of Illinois, 1838), which seems to survive in only one copy (WorldCat).
[18] In Greek mythology, the Sea People who were encountered around the Mediterranean basin when the Indo-Europeans invaded from the north and east. They may be identical with the Minoans or Phoenicians.

Fig. 5. Frontispiece from Rafinesque's
Analyse de la Nature **(Palermo, 1815).**
Transylvania University.

the name to the Atlantic ocean, and were first
populated by the Darans [from today's Maghreb] and

37

Corans[19] or Western Atlantes. Iceland was called Pushcara,[20] and was not settled, owing to the severe climate and awful volcanoes.

Numerous revolutions and invasions took place among those nations, until at last the Atlantes of Africa, united them all by conquest in one powerful empire, which extended over North Africa, Spain, France, Italy, part of Greece, Asia, &c.; and lasted many ages under several dynasties and emperors.

It was during the splendor of this empire, that America was discovered, by some bold navigators who were led by the trade winds, to the West Indies, in a few days from the Atlantic islands. They called them Antila Islands, which meant before the land, and America was called Atala or Great Atlantes. — Returning to the Azore land, by a north east course, they extolled the new country, and a great settlement was soon formed in Ayati or Ayacuta (Hayti) [the island of Hispaniola] and the neighboring continent by the Atlantes.

---

[19] = Kora, Senegalese, West African, possibly the Arabic-speaking founders of the Coree Indians in South Carolina.

[20] Sanskrit elements *prush* "ice, frost" + *ku* "earth, land."

Rafinesque goes on to introduce the Kutans, a Semitic people:

The Atalans, or American Atlantes spread themselves through North and South America, in the most fertile spots, but the marshy plains of Orenoe [Orinoco River in Venezuela, Guyana and Brazil], Maranon [northern Peru], Paraguay, and Mississippi; as well as the volcanoes of Peru, Chili, Quito, Guatimala and Anahuac [Mexico and Central America], prevented them from settling those parts of the continent. Many of the subjects of the Atlantic empire, such as the Tubalans,[21] Cantabrians, Cyclops and Cunetans [Canaanites], follow the Atalans in America, and become the Cutan nations.

It is difficult to trace the American nations, who have sprung from those early settlers, owing to the numerous revolutions and intermixtures which they have undergone: nor is it my intention to give now a complete genealogy of the Atalan and Cutan nations. I must confine myself to North America or even Kentucky.

---

[21] Descendants of Tubal (Gen. 10:2), believed to have populated the region south of the Black Sea from whence they spread north and east.

The Allegheny mountains were called Localoca [White Mountains]. Beyond them the country was called Great White Land, (Mahasweta-Bhumi of Hind:) and it became the seat of a great empire or the Western Atlantic Empire. This included of course Kentucky, but extended from lake Ontario in the north, to the Mississippi. The Atlantic shores called Locuta [White Places?], or Lachacuta [Seaside Places?] not settled, owing to their arid soil, lately emerged from the sea. This western empire may be called the Atalan empire.

Cherokee traditions maintain that their nation was formed by two strains of people, the *ani-yvwiyah* or Real People later joined by the Keetoowah (*kituwa, ani-giduhwa*), a word which can be traced to Hebrew K-T-B כתב "write," hence "people of the writing, or covenant."[22] Today, the

---

[22] Photographs of the Keetoowah Society in Indian Territory emphasize their legitimacy by showing the chiefs holding wampum belts. Ki-tu-wa in Cherokee has no meaning beyond the self-referential one but seems to be cognate with *ga-do-hi* "soil," *ga-du-hv* "town," and *ga-du* "bread." My argument for *kituwa* revolves around the fact that the Tsalagi language has no sound for b and renders it with *(wa)*. In volume 2 of *In Plain Sight*, Gloria Farley will present an interpretation of the "Possum Creek Stone" linking Sequoyah and the symbols on the thin gold plates of the original writing system to Cypriot. The four syllables seem to spell *ho-ni-ka-sa* ("to the victor"). "So the Taliwa tribe had apparently come to

United Keetoowah Tribe in Arkansas/Oklahoma forms a separate (and rival) entity from the Cherokee Nation of Oklahoma and Eastern Band of Cherokee Indians.[23] When Rafinesque's friend, the naturalist Thomas Nuttall, visited them in 1819, the Keetoowah were already partially removed and living in Arkansas. In 1996, the Eastern Band on the Qualla Reserve in North Carolina paid $3 million to acquire a 309-acre adjacent tract

America from the Mediterranean area centuries before Dr. Fell could read the Cherokee writing on the basis of the Cypriot script,c she writes (personal communication, November 4, 2003.). Barry Fell had identified Sequoyah's writing as "Linear C" in 1977 (*Ancient Vermont*, ed. Warren W. Cook, Academy Books of Castleton State College, Rutland, Vt., 1978). In Traveller Bird's account by descendants in *Tell Them They Lie* (Los Angeles: Westernlore Publishers, 1971), Sequoyah is linked to the ancient Seven Clan Scribe Society. This seems to be identical with the Keetoowah Society. Rafinesque seems to regard the word Kutan as representing "the Men," from supposed roots *ku* "men" and *tu* "land," an etymology similar to Atlas and Atlantic. But based on what linguist Mary LeCron Foster calls Proto-Pelagian, the root of Kutan and Keetoowah (if related) may be **qw(a)-* "build/construct," as seen in Egyptian *qs*, *qd*, Quechua *qorikán□ a*, *qósqo* "Cusco,", Hindu *kúta* "walls and houses made in part or whole of cement or mortar," and Iberian *kuta*, "a fortification, a defensive wall" ("The Transoceanic Trail: The Proto-Pelagian Language Phylum," *Pre-Columbiana* 1/1-2:88-113 at 98). Foster seems to miss the possibility that Quechua itself, the name for "language," is related.

[23] See *The United Keetoowah Band of Cherokee Indians in Oklahoma*, by Georgia Rae Leeds, 1999.

that contained an archeological site believed to represent the birthplace of the ancient priesthood of the Kituwah.[24]

We may hence identify Rafinesque's Atalans with the Appalachian Cherokee settlement and his Kutans with the Keetoowah, both originally from the Mediterranean and Northern Africa/Iberian region.

Rafinesque completes his picture of these "Old World Indians," as they might be called, by narrating what happened to them after the great Asian invasions of the Uto-Aztecan and Algonquian tribes:

> Before the Christian era a casual intercourse was kept up between the two continents. The Phenicians and Gadesiems [ancient "Punic" people of Cadiz, centered on the Biblical port of Tarshish] traded to America: this continent was known to the maritime nations of West Europe and North-west Africa. The Numidians went there 2000 years ago, as well as the Celts; they frequented Paria and Hayti principally. The Etruscans, a powerful nation of Italy, who settled there from the Rhetian Alps about three thousand years ago, went to America and wanted to send colonies there, but were prevented by the

---

[24]Associated Press, "Cherokees to Decide Fate of Sacred Land," June 5, 2001.

42

Carthaginians. This intercourse gradually declined, owing to the numerous shipwrecks and warlike habits of the Caribs, Iztacans and Oguzians, till the knowledge of America became almost lost or clouded in fables and legends.

During the decline of the Atalans, some fled to Anahuac and South America, where they founded new empires, or civilized many nations, such as the Cholulans [Toltec] of Anahuac, and the Muyseas [Muzo of Colombia], Puruays [Paraguayan Indians], Collaos [Aymara of Andean area], Tiahuanacos [Incan] and Cojas [Quechua] of South America, who ascribe their ancient civilization to white and bearded strangers.

Thus the ancient arts and sciences of North America were transferred to the South. In the greatest splendor of the Atalans and Cutans, they had built above one thousand towns on the waters of the Ohio, of which nearly two hundred were in Kentucky, and the remains of above one hundred are seen to this day. The population must have been as great as the actual one, and Kentucky must have had half a million of inhabitants at least. The monuments of these early nations are easily distinguished from the subsequent Iztacan monuments by a greater antiquity, their circular, elliptical and conical shapes.

43

I have quoted Rafinesque's work *in extenso* to show how far ahead of his times he was, for he lived in a day before cultural anthropology, ethnography, linguistics, archeology, or genetics had been invented. As we will see, his account of several millennia of American Indian history was surprisingly sound, both in its overall scope and themes, as well as in many details.

Rafinesque's information probably came primarily from Shawnee sources, but it is interesting that Choctaw oral tradition confirms what he had to say about the first Americans. According to a tradition recorded by Cushman, when the first Choctaws crossed the Mississippi from the west and arrived in their present homeland in the Southeast, they found a race of white giants whom they had to defeat. They used the same word for these forerunners of their nation and the European settlers who came many years later.

The emerging story of genetics supports a multiethnic outline of native history.

4 *Scholars and Savages*

WITH WIT and elegance, Professor Cyclone Covey of Wake Forest University catalogues many of the recent scholarly battles in pre-Columbian history. Noting that there were forebears to Clovis in the so-called Sandia style (like Clovis, also found in New Mexico), he suggested that Sandia shouldered points corresponded to Epigravettian and Solutrean in Europe. After all, the aesthetic care lavished on Clovis points presupposed some sort of background. Clovis did not come from a western direction (Siberia). The fact that eastern finds far outnumbered western suggested a different origin, logically European since the "greatest diversity equaled source.[25]" Clovis was simply the American manifestation of the Magdalenian and Aurignacian in France, from the same Cro-Magnon hunting culture responsible for the beautiful

---

[25] The latest archeology textbook supports Covey. "There is in fact good reason to believe that Clovis is a southeastern US original.... It follows that Clovis populations in the Southeast had centuries of experience in the region under their collective cultural belt. The incredible number of Clovis points found in places like the middle Tennessee River valley argues convincingly for [an Eastern US home for the culture]" (Pauketat and Loren 2005 p. 182).

Lascaux cave paintings (Covey 2004 pp. 42-58). In a chapter titled "Before Clovis, Indefinitely," Covey went even further. He drew attention to human tools and bones excavated in Puebla in the Valsequillo region of Mexico, dated to the Paleolithic and even Pleistocene epochs, long before the First Americans were supposed to have arrived according to academic timetables (pp. 58-62). Denigrators argued with the stratigraphic record. "Translation: Irreproachable consistent science by top scientists must not trump conventional premise" (p. 61). The government of Mexico confiscated the collection and whisked it out of sight (p. 60). In an ironic footnote, the world was mildly shocked on July 7, 2005 to read headlines about 60,000 year old human footprints from this same site.

"Conventional anthropologists cannot yet envision habitation dates for America comparable to European sites" (p. 61), nor can they admit that human beings might have crossed the ocean before Columbus.[26] Were there really "canoes, dugout, and kayak-type boats painted in red or black

---

[26] Not to open the whole subject of diffusionism versus isolationism, we might quote just one remark from a North American archeology textbook to illustrate the attitude taken by most academicians, teachers, and educated people. In his chapter on Native American prehistory, Dean R. Snow speaks of the "fantastic claims for pre-Columbian migration to the New World that plague archeologists periodically" (Kehoe 1981, p. 5). The anthropological echo is loud and plain in, e.g., Harold E. Driver, *Indians of North America* (Chicago, 1961).

in Pleistocene Spanish caves at La Pasiege, Castillo, and La Pileta, including the midship peak distinctive of Beothuk boats" (p. 57)? No, not boats, and if they were, not seaworthy. Elephant trunks appeared sculpted in the ball court at Chichen Itza? No, rather parrot beaks. Evidence had accumulated of fire-rings, smashed skulls of extinct animals, and primitive tools from 40,000 years ago – and even 400,000 – in California? Due to natural lightning strikes. The logic dismissing all these smoking guns reminds me of suicides killing themselves by the application of gunshot to the back of the head.

"There is no reason to believe, because America has been but recently discovered, that therefore, it has been but recently peopled," wrote an early ethnographer, before it became unfashionable (McIntosh in 1843). Several inscriptions tell of Phoenician visits to North America. A carving of the sea goddess Tanith was found deeply incised on a North Carolina boulder. Farley identified the deity's triangle dress and upraised forearms in Oklahoma, Kansas, Ohio, Vermont, Tennesse, New Mexico, Colorado, Nevada, California, and Mexico. The artifact called the Grave Creek Stone was removed from a depth of sixty feet inside a mound in West Virginia in 1838. It contained a Punic text from the first millennium B.C.E. The Bourne Stone discovered near Cape Cod has been interpreted as a declaration of Phoenician territorial claims along the East Coast. Fell translated the

Iberic text, "A Proclamation: By this Hanno takes possession." A similar inscription first recorded in 1780 from Rhode Island he rendered, "Voyagers from Tarshish this stone proclaims" (Thompson p. 149). "Minoans and Phoenicians were responsible for three major developments in Native American culture: the manufacture of bronze tools, the fabrication of stone buildings, and the first currency [oxhide-shaped tokens used for commerce]" (Thompson pp. 153, 157).

When Father Gregorio García wrote his book *The Origin of the Indians of the New World* (1607), he was struck by the immense racial diversity of Native Americans:

> The Indios come from many nations of the Old World.   Some are probably descended from the Carthaginians; some are descendants of the ten lost tribes of Israel; others come from Atlantis, Greece, Phoenicia and China" (Thompson 1992 p. 14).

Father Bernardino de Sahagun, author of the most complete description of the natives, agreed. He noted that the Mayas' own *Popol Vuh* told of a fleet of seven ships crewed by white-skinned, bearded people who arrived on their shores many centuries ago. His twelve- volume masterwork was deemed so dangerous it was suppressed. The heretical *Historia General de las cosas de Nueva España* did not see the light of day for several centuries.

One scholar has found hundreds of Semitic words he attributes to Phoenician influence in the core vocabulary of Quiché Maya. A verse-by-verse correspondence was demonstrated between Middle Eastern and Biblical creation stories and the Maya chronicle, *Popul Vuh*.[27] Noting that a learned Catholic priest by the name of Ximenez during the Spanish conquest in 1696 reported finding some books written with characters resembling Hebrew, the same scholar believed that "the Maya probably did use the old Phoenician alphabet for a time in the paleo-Americas [B.C.E.]" (Deal p. 7). "These were the three nations of the Quichés, and they came from where the sun rises [East]."[28] Furthermore,

> The Canaanite practice of infanticide, shunned by all other cultures of the Mediterranean during the classical Greek period, is clearly represented in the Americas. Worship of the sun god Ba'al (Bel) of the Canaanites is prevalent in the Americas even to this day. The Canaanite concept of the sun going into the earth for the night and out of the subterranean world

---

[27] David Allen Deal, *The Nexus. Spoken Language. The Link Between the Mayan and Semitic During Pre-Columbian Times* (Columbus, Ga.: ISAC Press, 1993).

[28] *Titulo de los Señores de Totanicapán*, p. 170, quoted in Deal, p. 18.

in the morning is evidenced in the Mexican/Spanish *entrada del sol* (entering of the sun—nightfall) and *salida del sol* (leaving of the sun—morning), exactly the opposite of European or so-called "western" thinking (p. 9).

Others surmise that Phoenician sailors and merchants from the heavily-traveled Indian Ocean spearheaded the conquest of the Pacific and were instrumental in the relatively late settlement of Polynesia, including Hawaii and New Zealand.[29] Phoenicians were among the ancient peoples claimed as forebears by Appalachian Melungeons. A highly publicized law case in 1872 proved that the daughter of a Melungeon mother in Chattanooga was descended from early Carthaginians and did not have Negro blood.[30] According to the young lawyer who defended the Melungeon daughter:

---

[29]Hurles, M.E. et al. (2003), "Native American Y chromosomes in Polynesia: the genetic impact of the Polynesian slave trade," American Journal of Human Genetics 72:1282-87; P. A. Underhill et al., "Maori Origins, Y-chromosome Haplotypes and Implications for Human History in the Pacific," *Human Mutation* 17:271-280; Thompson 1994 pp. 237-255.
[30] See Hirschman pp. 14-16.

[Her family] had high foreheads; long, straight, black hair, high cheek bones, thin lips, small feet with high insteps and prominent Roman noses, while the features of the Negro and mulatto were exactly the reverse of these.

In truth, these people belonged to a peculiar race, which settled in East Tennessee at an early day and in the vernacular of the country, they were known as "Melungeons." It was proven by the tradition amongst these people that they were descendants of the ancient Carthagenians; they were Phoenicians, who after Carthage was conquered by the Romans, and became a Roman province, emigrated across the Straits of Gibraltar and settled in Portugal (Hirschman pp. 18-19). . . .

The Carthaginian story is supported by genetic, archeological, anthropological, genealogical, and historical evidence, though interpreters vacillate about the age of the entry of people of Carthaginian descent into the Americas. Some say the Punic presence is of great antiquity, others assign it to the scattering of Jews and Moors from modern Portugal as a result of the Spanish Inquisition.

Before they developed the alphabet that evolved into our familiar Greek and Latin letters, the Phoenicians wrote in ogam, a peculiar finger language. Though it later resurfaces in

Celtic inscriptions in Ireland, the oldest specimens are found in North Africa and Spain.[31] Being the mixed, polyglot people that they were, Phoenicians adapted ogam to Celtic, Semitic, Berber, Libyan, Egyptian, Greek, and Germanic languages. It long continued in use as a favorite writing system, much as the Latin alphabet of the Phoenicians' supreme enemy did later.

And so, I photographed the Bandelier inscription, which I noticed included two crosses and a mask, and began to research its script.

Fig. 6. Bessie Cooper Yates, of Melungeon ancestry.

As mentioned, ogam had been known through stone inscriptions in Celtic lands for several centuries, but it was Barry Fell who first revealed its true origins. A key document was the

---

[31] Fell pp. 63-80.

short Ogam Tract added to the end of a medieval Celtic manuscript kept today in the library of Trinity College, Dublin. This often-overlooked treatise in the great Book of Ballymote illustrated specimens arranged geographically with Gaelic and Latin translations. Its rediscovery proved to be the Rosetta Stone for Phoenician languages. Fell was able through this link to decipher different versions of ogam in Libyan, Egyptian, Punic, Ibero-Celtic and a host of other Mediterranean languages (pp. 26-36). For instance, a script called African by the Ballymote scribe was an Iberian variety used by Phoenician speakers in southern Spain during the first millennium B.C.E. (p. 58). He published a chart comparing the oldest styles, which he dated from 800 B.C.E. onwards, with the fully developed Irish style of the Middle Ages (p. 52). Significantly, it was Old Ogam, distinguished by its lack of vowels, that predominated in America. Fell and his colleagues in the Epigraphic Society found it throughout New England, on stone buildings, gravestones, temple objects, and boundary markers (pp. 45-62). Predictably, these discoveries were widely ridiculed. Archeology students were cautioned by their professors not to cite *anything* that appeared to be prehistoric writing in America.

Ever since Major John Wesley Powell directed the Smithsonian's Bureau of Ethnology in the late 1800s, there had been a ban on investigations of this sort. It was, and to a degree still is, a firm policy. Thou shalt not seriously investigate any site in the Americas that bears any evidence of pre-Columbian cultural influence between the Old and New World. This approach reached the zenith of absurdity in a notable episode involving artifacts from Hopewell mounds in Michigan. In November 1896, Jacob Brown and George Rowe were hunting deer on Michigan's Upper Peninsula when they scared up a mink, which ran for the swamp and hid in a hollow stump:

> Digging for the mink, the men unearthed four stones, one of them the brownstone Newberry Tablet [later studied by Henriette Mertz] marked off in 140 approximately 1½" squares, each containing a foreign letter. The Smithsonian could make no sense of it. . . . [Mertz] printed it in *The Wine Dark Sea* [1964], where Fell spotted [it] . . . and deciphered [it] as a Cypro-Minoan bird divination (Covey 2001 p. 50) . . . .[32]

The University of Michigan was made custodian of these and more than 5,000 similarly inscribed artifacts. Within a few years, authorities destroyed all as fakes "since no literate person could have got to Michigan before Columbus (who never got there)." This act was labeled "obtuse criminal

---

[32] ESOP 4/218 pp. 132-36.

destruction of evidence" (Covey p. 50), but even more extreme cases are on record. It was thus no shock to us that among the hundreds of books and surveys and dissertations about Bandelier, no one had seen fit to comment on the writing outside Quetzalcoatl's Cave.

Months after my visit, I was able to read the inscription (from right to left, in the fashion of Hebrew) as: Q-H-T-Z-H-L C-TL-H-TL-H. The marks were in a style similar to a specimen discovered on Manana Island, near Monhegan Island, on the coast of Maine. Hinged Ogam was a variety of Bronze Age ogam lacking vowels, a predecessor of no. 16 of the Irish Ogam Tract. The Manana stone said: "Ships from Phoenicia, Cargo platform" (Fell p. 58). It then hit me that I had visited a place where the gods were buried, or at least one of them.

Still later in our visits to sacred places in the Southwest, we found the mother lode of ogam, just where one would expect to find it, on Inscription Rock. This imposing *cuesta* between Acoma and Zuñi contains all the boastful conquistador graffiti a historian could ever hope to see in one place. Every flourish has been catalogued. But what about the older and more numerous examples of ogam, all in plain sight? Although these are generally ignored, we read in our tour guide that Inscription Rock was called by the Indians "Place of the Strange Writings." This was before the first Spaniard cut his name on it with his dagger. We translated one of the inscriptions with a friend's help. It was Arabic, and it said, "For devotion."

Fig. 7. Tomb of Quetzalcoatl. The inscription begins with a cross and five strokes standing for the sound Q.

5 Chaco Canyon

QUETZALCOATL is unique in the pantheon of Mesoamerican deities in having both a beginning and an end, an arrival and departure, a birth and a death. He appeared as a culture-bearer in a ship from the East, bearded, flaxen-haired, white, and wearing a distinctive conical hat. When he later sailed off toward the rising sun, legends arose of his return. Moctezuma, the last emperor of Mexico at the time of the Spanish entrada, thought the foreigners returning white gods. In the same way, the Hopi look for the return of their long lost Elder Brother (*bahana*), who will bring the missing piece of the tablets of instructions. We have images of Queztlcoatl in the rock art record of the American Southwest. On balance, it was not surprising to find him at Bandelier.

The three classic sites of Mesa Verde, Chaco Canyon, and Casas Grandes are now understood as successive capitals of the same culture, flourishing between about 1000 and 1350 C.E. All lie on the same north-south meridian. The entire Southwest came under the domination of Mexican civilization about 1000. This transition is shown by the adoption of corn agriculture, distinctive art forms, pottery, and numerous other influences. It was a peaceful conquest, apparently, one to be

57

attributed to "the arrival of merchant or *pochteca* groups from West Mexico, heavily under Toltec influence."[33] One of the cultural hallmarks of the cities to the South was Quetzlcoatl: "These economic endeavors on the northern frontier of Mexico were associated with missionary activities of certain Mesoamerican cults of the gods, Tezcatlipoca, Quetzalcoatl, and Huitzilopochtli successively, each cult with its own identifiable trait cluster" (Schaafsma 1986 citing Di Peso 1974).

The so-called Jornada Style of rock art and pottery decoration includes numerous representations of Quetzalcoatl. Along with him appears another important Mesoamerican god, Tlaloc, the goggle-eyed rain god. Tlaloc is thought to be the chief deity represented in Hopi and Pueblo katsinas, the rain-bringer who one time demanded human sacrifice (p. 237). Quetzalcoatl is affiliated with fish, travel, trade, agriculture, and fertility.

Another major and widely venerated Mexican figure making an appearance in the north is Quetzalcoatl, the feathered serpent. He was

---

[33] Polly Schaafsma, *Indian Rock Art of the Southwest* (Albuquerque, N.M.: University of New Mexico Press, 1980) p. 198.

.

frequently associated with Tlaloc in Mexico and even shared some his characteristics. This deity... was recognized as the god of life, the morning, fertility, and agriculture and the the patron of twins and monsters. As the god of wisdom, calendars, and learning, he was the god of civilization... He occurs in the Mexican iconographic system in both anthropomorphic and serpent form, and he is also symbolized by the morning star, often in the form of an outline cross (Villagra 1954:80). In human form he may be bearded... Tozzer (1957:519) notes that the pointed hat, a Haustec feature, is among Quetzalcoatl's usual articles of attire... (p. 238).

Quetzalcoatl became the Horned or Plumed Water Serpent of the Pueblos, patron of rivers, springs, and irrigation. He is "recognizable through personality and costume in the Hopi Sky God, Sotuqnang-u, who wears a single horn or high cone when masked, a hat shaped like a star when unmasked."[34] The mask is another emblem associated with these Toltec gods from the south. In their katsina rain-bringing rituals, Hopi and other Pueblo Indians incorporated both masks and crosses. Interestingly, there is a

---

[34] P. 238, citing Ellis and Hammack 1968:41.

shrine dedicated to the Ten Commandments in Hotevilla on Second Mesa.[35]

The author of the voluminous *Conquest of Mexico* was a most exacting historian. He is a great authority. According to Prescott, Quetzalcoatl, whose Maya name was Kukulcán, instructed Mexico's natives "in the use of metals, in agriculture and in the arts of government (laws). . . it was the 'golden age' of Anáhuac [Mexico] (Prescott, p. 39). Is it a coincidence that Moses is assigned the invention of metallurgy by Western tradition, as well as being depicted in religious iconography with horns? Deal thought the first white, bearded stranger among the Mexicans was named after the Hebrew patriarch. "There were eleven, known Tolteca, dynastic kings, named 'Quetzalcoatl.' This dynasty lasted almost up to the twelfth century A.D. and the irruption into Anáhuac of the Azteca hordes in 1325 A.D. When the Azteca arrived they sought out Tolteca families, with whom a royal mating might take place. They found only eleven Tolteca families in all Anáhuac" (p. 33). Infamously, one of the invaders demanded a bride from the humiliated Toltecs and when her father visited wore her flayed skin as a wedding gift.

Deal also equated the *Popol Vuh*'s Balam Ak'ab with "the lords of Jacob, Israel," a suggestion Gordon guardedly

---

[35] Dan Evehema, *The Hotevilla Hopi Shrine of the Covenant* (New York: Marlowe & Co., 1995).

called "thought provoking." Among Deal's many other correspondences, the supposed similarity of the word Maya itself with Hebrew *mayah*, a root seen in our word "myriad," and thus stamping them as "the number people, mathematicians," has got to be controversial (p. 70). Reconstructing Quetzalcoatl's name in Hebrew, Deal obtained: Kay-tseh al ko-ah tale "man god banished to distant shore" (p. 75). Tlaloc (Chac in Maya) is Hebrew, phonetically *shaw-ag* (p. 78). Gordon had encouraged Deal's researches, writing to him, "From the contents of the Popol Vuh I concluded, nearly twenty-five years ago, that a common Near East [Middle Eastern] source underlies it and the early chapters of Genesis" (p. 102). Personally, my favorite loan-word from Hebrew into Mexican is *tamale* "Aztec food,"[36] derived from *tah male*, "little chamber. . . filled, be full": I thought immediately of kugels and blintzes.

The hat standing for supernatural power is without a doubt the characteristic sailor's cap discovered on several American rock carvings cross-referenced to contemporary Phoenican iconography by Farley.[37] Originating in Sumeria

---

[36] Alfonso Caso, *The Aztecs; the People of the Sun* (University of Oklahoma Press 1958); cf. Deal p. 116.

[37] A petroglyph of a figure in a reed boat at Maba's Shelter in eastern Oklahoma shows the helmsman wearing a brimmed, high-

(where many believe the first Phoenicians came from), the "wizard's hat" retained its symbolism and popularity for centuries. It was adapted by the Celts and Germans, the latter adding familiar horns. Perhaps the strangest change it suffered was being fashioned into the bishop's mitre, this, too, a symbol of holiness.

Chaco Canyon is a complex of ruins on the other side of the Jemez Mountains from Bandelier. It is equally associated with Anasazi or Ancestral Pueblo history, assigned to the period between about 1000 and 1250. In 1990, it was designated a World Heritage Park. Lying at latitude 36° N, longitude 108° W, at an elevation exactly one mile high, the bone-dry red rock canyon is situated squarely in the center of the San Juan River drainage area, dominated today by Navajo and Apache Indian reservations. Chaco Wash is a deeply etched *arroyo* flowing only after heavy rains, when streams of water also jet down the walls of the mesa into the village. The growing season here is short, always less than 150 days and often less than 100 days — not a productive place for corn. Wood resources are scarce, and the surrounding desert offers only rare clumps of grass, pygmy juniper and rabbitbush. An 18-mile stretch of washboard dirt road takes you into the site, across a perfectly flat, totally unremarkable landscape.

---

crowned hat similar to the mosaic of a sailor from ancient Tripoli in Libya (Farley 1994, p. 43).

According to a consensus of archeologists, climate in centuries when Chaco Culture prospered was not much different. So what is it doing here?

After an unintentional detour through the Jemez Mountains, we arrived at Chaco late in the day. By the time Fajada Butte came into view and we checked in at the visitors center, it was 3 o'clock. The site closed at sunset. Incredibly, over a hundred visitors still lingered, including some Dutch backpackers and a yellow school bus full of what we learned were primarily grandmothers from Ohio, many with walkers. We went on the circuit road and parked at the first great house, Hungo Pavi (Reed Spring). The name is thought to be the same as Shungopavi, one of the mother villages of the Hopi on Second Mesa. As it turned out, we were to encounter many echoes and reminders of the Hopi. After touring the elevated kiva of Chetro Ketl, we walked along the Petroglyph Trail toward Pueblo Bonita, stopping to make tobacco offerings in the rock cup beside a figure we identified as a marker for one of our clans, Bird. A large croaking raven flew overhead.

Nothing prepared us for the eerie beauty of Pueblo Bonito. We stood on the overlook and the raven returned. The air brushed by his wing feathers filled our hearing like a whirlwind. Six smaller birds passed the same way. They all flew into a cliffhole over the Bird Clan marker. Later, we saw that the setting sun cast a shadow there that resembled a long-beaked raven looking over his shoulder on a perch. The Grandfather Raven disappeared into the top of the shadow's head, the "open door." We stood staring at the 700 rooms of Pueblo Bonito before descending and walking around.

It was a magical moment. But that was nothing to compare with the sight that greeted us as we rounded the D-shaped perimeter walls, some of them three stories high. Down a long ceremonial avenue leading back to Hungo Pavi stood the unmistakable figure of Kokopelli, the humpback flute player. There he was with his hunch, flute, and triangular hat or horn, and he seemed to be facing and dancing south. It was ten minutes to six, just before the sun dipped below the horizon. Everything was a golden red, with deep shadows. If we had not been delayed in our journey through the mountains we would not have arrived at the proper time to see the 100-foot-tall effigy (Fig. 8).

Archeologists have often remarked on Chaco's unusual groundplan. The city is laid out with straight, interconnecting streets, while all around it are roads, estates, mounds, gardens, and lookout points, making for elaborate lines of sight. "The dense network of roads in 'downtown' Chaco created redundant, parallel routes clearly unnecessary for pedestrian functions," noted one archeologist (Stephen Lekson in Pauketat and Loren p. 244-45). The city was obviously a great trade center. An estimated 100,000 pieces of turquoise beads from the Cerillos mines south of Santa Fe, 35 copper bells, about 35 skeletons of scarlet macaws from Mexico, and 180 great cylinder vases were recovered in excavations (p. 246). The Great Houses set in the countryside surrounding Chaco's kivas, storage rooms, merchant arcades, and palace were obviously elements of a planned city that mirrored the Chacoan world order. But whose order was it?

I suggest Chaco was built as it was, and where it was, because of the striking shadow of Kokopelli on the canyon wall. Kokopelli, like Quetzalcoatl, was a rain-bringer, culture bearer, and tradesman. Schaafsma describes him as "a character with multiple but interrelated attributes. . . an ithyphallic being with a hump. . . with antenna and other insect features. . . a rain priest who calls the clouds and moisture with his flute" (p. 140). "His favorite pastime. . . is seducing maidens, and his hump is said to be filled with babies, blankets, or seeds, some of which he gives to each girl he seduces" (pp. 140-1).

The gates and walls of Pueblo Bonito emphasized and left unspoiled the vista of the city's patron saint. This can only be seen from one angle, with the setting sun behind you. Another such great shadow appears on the north wall, and significantly, nothing was built in front of it either. Its shape profiles a gigantic raven (Fig. 9). Another titanic shadow loomed at the end of the avenue skirting Chetro Ketl, though I do not pretend to know what it represented. . . a pipe-carrier? Thus the cityscape was symbolically adapted to the landscape. Its ruler may even have styled himself Kokopelli. The "elite" individuals found buried in Pueblo Bonito were foreign rulers who used the locals as slave labor. Navajo traditions called its builder the Gambler: Gambling was a favorite pastime of Kokopelli. Evidently, like Quetzalcoatl, Kokopelli was a *puchteca*. These forerunners of the conquistadors were noblemen commissioned by Mesoamerican kings to find and exploit distant, simpler societies.

Cosmopolitan Chaco "lasted perhaps little over six decades" in the eleventh century, with the successor sites of Aztec to the north and Casas Grandes in Chihuahua to the south "at maximum...six centuries." After the Pueblo Indians had shaken off this autocratic hierarchy, they retained memories of Chaco as a dark place, ruled by "a people who had enormous amounts of power: spiritual power and power over people." The shadows of Chaco Canyon were responsible for a determined egalitarianism in tribal affairs down to the present day (Lekson pp. 268). The reason Kokopelli is often shown in a recumbent position (Schaafsma p. 140) is not because he is in bed, but because he is dead. This is the conventional way to signify a person's death in petroglyphs. In my opinion, these representations celebrate the overthrow of the Bow Clan and technologically-inclined Flute Society associated with a foreign god. "When complexity left the Colorado Plateau and the homelands of

the modern Pueblos, the people who stayed behind created new cultural controls – social structures, ceremonial systems – to make sure it would never happen again" (Lekson p. 269).

Fig. 8. View of Kokopelli figure in mesa cliff at end of east road from entrance to Pueblo Bonito just before sunset on a late summer day.

67

Fig. 9. The Raven at Chaco.

6 Apes and Elephants

BEFORE Chacho came Mimbres. Known to us primarily through their rich pottery series, Mimbreños are also believed to number among the ancestors of today's Pueblo Indians. They dwelt south of the Mogollon Rim in southern Arizona and New Mexico, concentrated eastward along the lower Rio Grande toward Texas. Mimbres Culture has always puzzled archeologists for its sophisticated art forms. It is a tradition that seems to have no precedent. Particularly inexplicable is a naturalistic depiction of deep-sea fishes, ibises, and other flora and fauna. None of these is indigenous to the American Southwest nor ever has been. This implies either the pottery ware, the pattern, or the artisans came from somewhere else.

One such Mimbres artifact belongs to the Museum of Indian Art and Culture in Santa Fe. It is a black-on-white funerary object, "killed" with a hole in the bottom like many similar specimens from Eastern Woodland burial mounds. The Santa Fe piece plainly shows four apes -- or at least, apelike figures which someone who had never seen an ape, only heard stories of them, might use (Fig. 10). So were elephants drawn in the margins of medieval manuscripts by

Fig. 10. This Mimbres figure has human hands, head and feet, plus a long ringtail (here depicted as a chain of rings, suggesting a misunderstood oral account). It may be compared with a human with rabbit tail on another piece. Both were probably attempts by descendants of ancient North African sea people in what is now New Mexico to reproduce creatures never seen by them, but indicative of their ancestors' place of origin. Item 16209, dated circa 1000-1150 C.E. *Courtesy Laboratory for Anthropology, Santa Fe, N.M.*

Northern European monks who had never laid eyes on the animal. Notoriously, there are no apes and never have been in the Americas. I believe Mimbres apes functioned in the same way as kangaroos in Hopi Sun Park, elephants in Chaco Canyon (Fig.11), and ibises and jackals in Colorado (Farley) — to remind future generations of their ancestors' countries of origin. A mound in Wisconsin and petroglyph in Barnesville, Ohio have been identified as likenesses of an extinct Moroccan elephant, the species used by Hannibal to attack Rome (Covey p. 34). Mimbres deep-sea fish, ibises, and Gibraltar-like apes once more implicate the Phoenicians. Among the unusual objects in the same case as the Mimbres pots in Sante Fe are sturdy, still-serviceable fishing nets, with interstices too large for any fish but those of the deep sea.

Not only were the Phoenicians, or at least, their heirs, present in the American Southwest and Mexico, but also Arabs, Egyptians and Berbers. Fell pointed out that the southwest's Zuñi people possessed a vocabulary close to Coptic, and that the Pima language was Semitic. In fact, the name Hohokam, designating the Southwest's first advanced culture, was probably Libyan. And we have already seen how Inscription Rock contains specimens of archaic Arabic.

In Hopi traditions, the sky divinity Cotukinungwa is "Chief of All," but he is not the same as a living god. This role is occupied by Masau'u, their leader and guardian. Masau'u was the original occupant of the land who gave the

Hopi stone tablets and permission to reside in his territory. They had arrived from the flood-destroyed previous world on reeds (perhaps Polynesian-style stick maps), crossing the Pacific Ocean on stepping-stone islands that sank behind them. Presumably they coasted Baja California before sailing into the Gulf of California and landing at the mouth of the Colorado River, a sacred site where boys even today must race to collect salt in order to become men in their clans. The Hopi regard the Grand Canyon as their place of emergence. Masau'u is described as a tall black man with either ugly or very beautiful features, and several people have commented on the similarity of the name to Africa's Masaai people. (The word means "The People" in their own language.) Let us see what Masau'u's territory consisted of:

> Masau'u first traveled south, then circuitously to the eastward until he reached his starting point. He called this area his land. The exact limits are unknown, but it is surmised he started from a point about where Fort Mojave now is situated, thence south as far as the Isthmus of Panama, skirted eastward along the Gulf of Mexico and northward by the line of the Rio Grande up into Colorado, thence westerly along the

Fig. 11. Complete with trunk, flapping ears and short tail, an elephant is carved in bas-relief on the cliffside at Chaco Canyon. The labyrinth to the left probably depicts the people's emergence. The symbol may represent a tribal memory of a passage to India or original homeland in Africa. It is certainly naturalistic.

thirty-sixth parallel or thereabouts to the Rio Colorado, meandering along its course and so on southward to his starting point at Fort Mojave. This was Masau'u's land originally (*Hopi Tales*, 55-57).

Strengthening the supposition that Mesoamerica was first colonized from Africa are the colossal Vera Cruz heads with thick lips, bold chins, and flat noses. One may add African admixture evident in ancient Olmecs, Toltecs, and

73

Aztecs.[38] The Zuñi tribe, coeval with the Hopis if not older, brought the North African word "adobe" to the Southwest and divided its own villagers into two moieties, one black and one red. Zuni contains such a high degree of mutual intelligibility with Coptic that it can be considered an African language. Mills finds abundant parallels to Egyptian practices in Hopi mythology, though he believes Massau'u is rather to be identified with Moses and the Red Sea port of Massawa, a crossing point to Arabia (Mills 1998). Today's Abiquiu in northern New Mexico is a crypto-Muslim pueblo whose Arabic church services may go back farther than the self-mutilating Catholic Penitentes. The village (Fig. 12) began as early as 1598, when it was garrisoned as the northern outpost of New Spain. It was repeopled with Genizaros in 1735, bringing together ex-slaves, half-breeds, renegades, and other outcasts.

Between 700 and 1200 C.E., Muslims and Moors of the Mediterranean had the world's highest standard of living, its greatest merchant fleets, and the most advanced seats of learning anywhere. Muslim geographers also maintained the most comprehensive maps in existence; one of them showed the coastline of Antarctica. Al-Masudi's Historical Annals of 942 C.E. records an unusual sea voyage of the 10th century, when a ship under the command of Captain Khashkhash

---

[38] Thompson pp. 91-105; Covey 2004 p. 114.

(probably a Babylonian) set sail from Cordova, Spain. After a long journey west across the Atlantic, it returned laden with treasures. The only possible destination it could have visited

Fig. 12. The Penitente Morada at Abiquiu. Nearby are Muslim-style graves, as identified by grave fences and mounds of raised, cleared dirt.

was North America. In the 12th century, Europeans knew the Atlantic as the "Sea of Darkness" and believed they they would fall off the earth if they tried to cross it. The contemporaneous Arabic geographer Al-Idrisi knew better. He told of one voyage by the Brothers Al-Mugrurim who

75

sailed for about a month – the same time it took Columbus to reach the Antilles 350 years later following the same trade winds – before reaching a land "inhabited with Berbers and sheep" (Thompson p. 289). The Chinese Sung dynasty historians also recorded the Moors' westward embarkations from the Biblical port of Tarshish, or Tartessos, which they called Tashish (pp. 290-1).

Surprisingly, Spanish rulers did not place the same restrictions on Muslims as they did on Jews. Much greater latitude was given to the Moors who remained in Spain after 1492. They were allowed to retain their language (Arabic) and to emigrate at will to the New World. Jews were forbidden to use Hebrew or depart for any Christian country. Moreover, Moslem religious authorities were extremely liberal in their rulings, even allowing Moriscos to take the required oaths before Catholic authorities in a feigning manner.[39] In fact, several old Jewish families managed to elude the Inquisition by dissembling Islam. For these reasons, despite their lower numbers, crypto-Muslims may outnumber crypto-Jews proportionately in New Mexico, and some crypto-Muslims may actually be crypto-Jews.

---

[39] L.P. Harvey, *Muslims in Spain 1500-1614* (Chicago: University of Chicago, 2005).

7 Los Quelites

ACCORDING TO our *chueta*, the exact spot surrounding what he prefers to call the Covenant Stone was awarded to twenty families from Tomé and Los Chaves, just east of there. Chartered as San Francisco del Valle, the grant was made by Governor Del Valle in 1761. In the well-known map by Don Bernardo de Miera Y Pacheco of 1779 there is a village right on this hill called Los Quelites, which is Spanish for the wild herb called lambs-quarters. "Our Jewish ancestors were very secretive and they enjoyed sophisticated puns," he said. The reason they chose that word was its association with the paschal lamb. Pesach was celebrated on the tableland above the Decalogue Stone (see cover), until authorities suppressed the heretical enclave and broke their altar in two (Fig. 13). As for Chaves, this is a classic Spanish-Portuguese Jewish name. Congregants greet each other at temple with the salutation, "Shavres," meaning "comrade, friend." The expression passed into Yinglish (Yiddish English) in the phrase "little shaver." "There is a story that the Sephardic ancestors who settled in Tomé and Los Chaves in the early 1700s had a division among themselves," he continued. "Some wanted to continue their Jewish ways, and others wanted to abandon

77

them for Christianity only. The faithful Jews left to form Los Quelites, and eventually Seboyetta."

So did the Spanish Judaizers of the early 1700s carve the Decalogue Stone? I do not believe so. For one, the writing contains unusual orthographic features that could never have been known to them. For another, Gordon, a Semitic expert, has precisely dated the style of punctuation to seventh or eighth century Byzantium. While serving as a visiting professor at the University of New Mexico, he made two excursions to inspect the stone. He described it as "an abridged version of the Ten Commandments in the old Phoenician/Hebrew letter-forms" (Deal p. 1). Could modern-day Spanish Jews have known Phoenician letter-forms? Possibly, but it is unlikely. An earlier timeframe for the inscription was indicated by a report by geologist George Morehouse, who judged that the heavy patina on the surface of the stone was of an age between 500 and 2,000 years old (Thompson p. 181).

In 1993, the Gordons visited the Israeli Archeological Museum in Jerusalem. Connie Gordon, a Middle Eastern scholar like her husband, spotted two stone slabs inscribed with the Ten Commandments in Samaritan. The team learned that instead of the Jewish Mezuzah affixed to doorways to ward off evil, and proclaim Jewish faith, the Samaritans employed decalogue stones. They located two such stones in the museum's collection, one found at Schechem, or Nablus, dated third to fourth century C.E., and another found at Tel Bilu, near Rehovot, south of Tel Aviv, dated sixth or seventh century. Gordon went on to write:

> We are not dealing with a modern forgery. It has been there as far back as the local inhabitants (Indian as well as White) knew. The Whites have witnessed it since about 1800. The Indians call the place "The Cliff of the Strange Writings. . . . The question arises as to what route the carriers of "Samaritan" culture took to reach Los Lunas. The latter site is near the Rio Puercos [Pigs], a tributary of the Rio Grande. This suggests that the route from Palestine was through the Mediterranean and the Atlantic, then into the gulf of Mexico, up the Rio Grande, and finally up the Rio Puercos to Los Lunas (Hidden Mountain) (Gordon in Deal p. 2).

Why are such monuments ignored? Stephen Jett, a Johns Hopkins-trained professor of geography at the University of California in Davis, believes it is because of political correctness and reverse racism. Toe-the-line academicians will not look at evidence for transoceanic contact because they view the hypothesis of diffusionism as injurious toward "our Native Americans." The attitude is part and parcel with imperialism, the white man's burden, and colonial mentalities; it is "patronizing and intellectually unjustifiable," according to Jett. Lakota Sioux lawyer and philosopher Vine Deloria, the late professor of law at the University of Colorado in Boulder, has pointed out how the Indian must be vigilantly "re-Indianized" so that he will be acceptable to white anthropologists and remain the preserve of those who "study" him (*God Is Red; White Lies, Red Earth*, notably in the essay "Anthropologists and Other Friends"). The public is ill served by such an obscurantist schism. Like

Fig. 13. This smashed stone was probably the altar of crypto-Jews celebrating Passover and other services above Los Quelites. The inscription reads ABAI, Aramaic/Greek for "teachers, fathers."

the Decalogue Stone itself, the desecrated altar of New Mexican pioneers on Hidden Mountain is protected only by its own mystery. Government officials do nothing to secure or guard these antiquities for future generations, and they are vulnerable to more than scholarly neglect. As the Roman poet Juvenal quipped, "Who will guard the guards (*Quis custodiet custodes*)?

In 1839, not far from Copacabana Beach in Rio de Janeiro, Juan de Cunha Barboza discovered a giant inscription three thousand feet up a perpendicular cliff. The letters were already badly worn and have now almost disappeared. Read by Bernardo da Silva Ramos in 1921, they yielded amazing evidence of visits by Phoenicians and Hebrews from the ninth century B.C.E. In plain sight of all sailing vessels, "Badezir, son of Jethbaal, from Tyre, Phoenicia" had had his name inscribed (Covey 2004 p. 113). This was an age when Jews in Jerusalem hired Phoenician mercenaries from Tyre to travel to a land called Ophir. According to the Bible, Ophir was the location of King Solomon's gold mines. It required three years for the round-trip voyage, which went around the Cape of Good Hope. Wealth obtained from New World mines played a major part in Solomon's building of the First Temple. A fourteenth-century Portuguese map carries a note that King Solomon's riches came from a land called Bracir, probably an early version of Brazil (Thompson pp. 145-6).

In 1872, a Brazilian rancher, Joaquin Alves da Costa, sent the Historical Institute in Rio de Janeiro a copy he had made of an inscription on four broken stones slaves had found on his property near the Paraíba River. Ladislau Netto, the director of the museum, struggled with the inscription's Phoenician language until he finally published the results of his research. The suggestion that the writing recorded a Phoenician expedition sailing from the Red Sea to Brazil unleashed a storm of official wrath around the world. According to his reconstruction, the Paraíba Text was from the sixth century B.C.E. and told of the voyage of merchants from Sidon:

> We are sons of Canaan from Sidon, the city of the king. Commerce has cast us on this distant shore, a land of mountains. We sacrificed a youth for the exalted gods and goddesses in the 19th year of Hiram—our mighty king. We embarked from Ezion-Geber into the Red Sea and voyaged with ten ships. We were at sea together for two years around the land belonging to Ham [Africa], but we were separated by a storm. We are no longer with our companions. So we have come here – twelve men and thirteen women – to this shore which I, the admiral, control. May the exalted gods and goddesses favor us (Revised

Translation after Cyrus Gordon in James Bailey, *The God Kings and the Titans*, 1973, p. 39).

The Paraíba Text was declared a fraud shortly after its publication, but subsequent scrutiny by scholars confirms that it is probably authentic. Passages questioned at first have been verified by identical inscriptions on Phoenician artifacts, including ancient formulae and grammatical forms unknown in the 1800s (Thompson p. 151). Most of the members of the expedition were very likely Jewish. In the meantime, though, it continues to be academic contraband. A debunker in 1968 called it "a pathetic mishmash of linguistic forms, or spellings and of scripts of various dates and places patched together from nineteenth-century handbooks," which Covey glossed as, "pedantry, conjecture, and presupposition." "Once again a reputable scholar out of animus against ancient ocean-crossings sought all his learned ingenuity to find a hypothetical forgery without considering the straightforward face-value message wholly consistent with itself and 6th-century-B.C. context" (Covey 2004 p. 113). In the meantime, the Brazilian rancher disappeared back into the jungle, along with the original stones. Today, it is impossible to determine how much is reconstruction and how much is genuine. The same fate overtook Rafinesque's precious original of the Walam Olum, a bunch of sticks thrown out in the trash upon his death.

83

8 The Petroglyphs on Hidden Mountain

THE PARAÍBA story has much in common with Calalus, another Jewish colony in the New World that skeptics dismiss as nonsense. In 1924, a hoard of gray-to-blue lead tablets was discovered in cement-like caliche near an abandoned limekiln eight miles northwest of Tucson, Arizona. Workers had found steel swords on the same spot in 1886. The site was excavated by field crews from the University of Arizona Museum. The inscriptions were published as the Calalus Texts. The crude plates told of a band of Hebrew refugees who fled Charlemagne's Frankish Christian regime and sailed across the Atlantic to a land known as Calalus, ruled by Silvanus Toltezus in his capital of Rhoda (Greek for "red," the name of an Aegean island, Rhodes).

True to form, many academics suspected a hoax. The official line issued by the University of Arizona after a $25,000 payoff "slandered all the honest people who had unearthed and studied what included hard-alloyed lead swords and spears." As Covey pointed out, "Amateurs can mold lead but do not know how to alloy, let alone reproduce forgotten ceremonial standards engraved with menorah and Hebrew tags like *shalom, qaddash, elohim, goi godol* (great nation)." Beside the names of the kings there were a menorah with seven burning candles, a pair of Hebrew chalices (*habdalah*), incense spoons, burning incense, numerals I to X in double column signifying the Ten Commandments, and words in carefully-drawn square Hebrew script.

We have seen above that without doubt contact did occur between Europe and the Mediterranean and the Americas reaching back to the Minoans and Egyptians. The Phoenicians were among the most energetic explorers of coastlines and river systems. The Western continent and its islands were known to Plato, Aristotle (or one of his pupils), Diodorus Siculus, Theopompus of Chios, Plutarch, Strabo, and Erastosthenes of Cyrene in Greco-Roman antiquity.[40]

During the 500-year *pax Romana*, Europeans seem to have lost interest in America, as mentioned by Rafinesque. The Romans were afraid of the open sea. Not being able to swim, they preferred to keep within sight of land (swimming was not revived as a sport until the Renaissance). Iron had replaced copper as the most desirable metal, and there was

[40] Aristotle, *De Mundo* (Venice, 1521), pp. 3, 392b; Peter Kalkavage, trans. Plato's Timaeus (Newburyport, Mass: Focus Publishing, 2001); Didorus Siculus, *Bibliotheca Historica*, trans. C. H. Oldfather (London: Heinemann, 1935) 9:19, 20; Aelian's *Varia Historica* (Cambridge, Mass.: Harvard University Press, 1997), 3:18; "Life of Sestorius," in *Plutarch's Lives*, trans. John and William Landhorne (London: Tegg, 1865) pp. 399-400; Strabo, *Geographica*, 2 vols., trans. H. L. Jones (London: Heinemann, 1917, 1923).

little need to visit foreign shores. Moreover, "voyages beyond the Empire were fraught with high costs, piracy, and uncertainty. . . . Caribbean gold, North American furs, and exotic plants were the only New World imports of substantial value. . . During an era of tranquility. . . the Empire's attention focused on...the eastern Mediterranean" (Thompson p. 162). Yet knowledge of the lands on the other side of the Atlantic persisted. Jordanes, the most important Gothic historian, writing in the middle of the sixth century, took it for granted: "The ocean has in its western region certain islands known to almost everyone by reason of the great number of those who journey to and fro."[41] The West Indies were visited regularly, so it is entirely within the realm of possibility that a group of Romans of the eighth century could have sailed for the Gulf of Mexico and made their way inland following the Rio Grande to present-day New Mexico and Arizona.

Properly understood, the Calalus Texts record a compelling history. There was a Jewish settlement in Toltec country that survived until about 900. The capital, Rhoda, which the Jews wrested from the Indian emperor, was described as fronting a large plain surrounded by hills. The description fits the Snake River valley where the plates were

---

[41] *De summa temporum de origine actibus gentis Romanorum* (Monumenta Germaniae Historiarum), 1:4, 7.

unearthed. Theodore, the colony's first leader, organized his confederation in Rome in 765, crossed the ocean, and attacked this Indian city, where he captured over 700 persons. He ruled for fourteen years, four of them in America. One scribe depicts him as bald. Also bald was his successor, Jacob, who came from Britain and ruled for six years. The next prince of Calalus ruled 17 years. Israel I, as he was styled, had been born on the Seine, perhaps in Paris, in 699 and lived to be 93 years old. The year 790 marked a decisive victory over the natives. King Israel appointed rabbis and presided over an assembly of consuls from allied cities. Calalus at this time could field 700 troops. Under Israel II, who reigned six years, war returned. The annalists tell of a later ruler who made the mistake of freeing the Toltecs. He was banished for this by the Sanhedrin. Returning from banishment, he attempted to subjugate them anew, but the Jews had to abandon their fields and villages and retreat within their walls. In 895, the scribe wrote, "3,000 killed, and the leader with his principal men captured." Next, he quoted Cicero and added, "It is uncertain how long life will continue." The final entry is dated 900: *Nil nisi cruce...venit summa dies et ineluctabile cruce tempus.* The deplorable Latin can be translated, "There remains nothing but torture. . . the final day has come, the unavoidable time for death" (Covey 23-24).

When the Calalus discovery was announced in the New York Times, the initial reaction of scholars from various disciplines was positive. In time, however, skeptics drew attention to the clumsy Latin, crude Christian emblems, use of the expression "anno Domini" (A.D.), and seemingly incongruous Masonic symbolism. Was it even possible that a colony of Europeans would speak Aramaic, Greek, Latin, Old French, and Anglo-Saxon all at the same time? Covey pointed out, "Bad Latin may prove better than disprove." He also found quotations from Cicero, Horace, Vergil, and Livy. The unique map of the colony was a sophisticated device, much like a coat of arms (Fig. 14). Its shape was echoed in the eight divisions (*shemona peoth*) carved in Hebrew down the stem of a *nehushtan* (Moses staff). Moreover, it plainly showed twelve sections.

If an army of eighth-century Jews traveled from Rome to modern-day Arizona or New Mexico, what kind of transport did they use? In 1985, a shipwreck was discovered about 20 miles south of Haifa at a depth of about six to ten feet, only 80 yards off the coast of the home of Elisha Linder, an Israeli who wrote his doctoral thesis under Cyrus Gordon. I met Dr. Linder at a meeting of the Epigraphic Society and Institute for the Study of American Cultures in Columbus, Georgia, in 2002. Named the Ma'agan Mikhael after the nearby kibbutz where it was found, the wreck proved one of

Fig. 14. The Calalus Cross. The sections within the large square probably stand for the twelve tribes of Israel dispersed between Byzantium, Gaul, Britain, and the Far West.

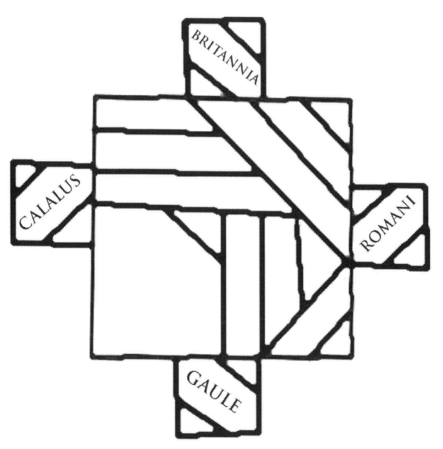

the best-preserved wooden-hulled ships ever discovered in the Mediterranean.

It was Dr. Linder's knowledge of the capabilities of ancient ships that served as the cornerstone for Gordon's 2000 book *A Scholar's Odyssey*. The pine hull of the ship is 43 feet long and about 13 feet wide. Its estimated displacement was 25 tons. A special museum was built to house the ship at Haifa University's Center for Maritime Studies. Plans are to build a replica and sail it around the Mediterranean as a traveling beacon of international peace. We asked Dr. Linder if the new Ma'agan Mikhael would be ocean-worthy? "Absolutely," came his reply. He said the next port of call would be New York. We believe a flotilla of such merchantmen may have been available to Theodore and his colonists setting forth from Rome in 775. The ships could have come through the Indian Ocean and across the Pacific along sea lanes established by the Phoenicians and plied later by the Arabs just as easily as across the Atlantic.

What was taking place in Europe in the year 775? Charlemagne had just stormed Italy's capital, Pavia, assuming the title "King of the Lombards and Patrician of the Romans." He immured the last Lombard king in a monastic cell and marched triumphantly toward Rome in 774. Adrian I was pope, a Roman nobleman, son of Theodore (772-795 -- of the same family as the organizer of the expedition to Calalus?). Charlemagne's conquest of Italy and negotiations

90

with the Pope would result in the Donation of Constantine, a forgery that legitimized the Vatican, drove a wedge between the West and East, and inaugurated the Holy Roman Empire. The Frankish emperor was crowned in St. Peter's basilica on Christmas Day, 800. In 775, Spain was ruled by the Omayyads, Persia by the Abbasid caliphs, and Leo IV the Khazar was the Byzantine emperor. Britain was divided into numerous kingdoms, and the Saxons and Bavarians were in retreat from Charlemagne's armies, about to embrace Christianity. In the south of France, there was a Jewish state ruled by Babylonian princes allied and intermarried with the Carolingians (Zuckermann 1972). There was even a Judaic academy in Narbonne.

In Jewish history, the eighth century is the beginning of the period of the Geonim (singular, *gaon*):

> The seat of spiritual authority of the Jewish world was the yeshivah (academy). Between the eighth and eleventh centuries this was not simply a learning institute, but also the supreme court and source of instruction for all Jews. The head of the yeshivah, the gaon, was regarded as the highest religious authority, but his responsibilities also included organizing the courts, appointing judges and community leaders as well as scribes, ritual slaughterers and other officials (Barnavi p. 86).

91

It is certainly true that Jews enjoyed the privileges of Roman citizenship until the fall of the empire. Even after that, Jewish communities in Rome and Constantinople had special dispensations. In many countries, notably Muslim Spain and southern France, Jews were guaranteed the same rights as others. They were able to bear arms, own land, live wherever they pleased, conduct trade, worship in their homes or synagogues, and even hold public office. Charlemagne's father Pepin had made the founder of Narbonne, the Gaon Machir, his vassal. Machir gave his sister to Pepin and took the sister of Pepin as one of his wives. He belonged to the powerful Nasi family that later produced Doña Gracia, "The Woman who Defied Kings."[42]

---

[42] Beginning as Beatrice de Luna of the Marrano family of Miguis in Portugal, this remarkable Jewish heroine later ran the international banking concerns of her husband, Francisco Mendez, lived in Antwerp, London, Italy, Greece, and Istanbul, and became the richest woman in the world. She acquired a high standing with the Sultan in Kushta and he gave her the city of Tiberias in Ottoman Palestine to establish a refuge for the Jews. Tiberias was the city out of which it was said that "from it (Israel) will be redeemed and it will be the spiritual center for all Jewish communities in the Diaspora." Doña Gracia Nasi's Tiberian colony was an important forerunner of the modern state of Israel. See Andrée Aelion Brooks, *The Woman Who Defied Kings. The Life and Times of Doña Gracia Nasi* (St. Paul, Minn.: Paragon Press, 2002).

Esther Benbassa's *The Jews of France* is the most complete and well-documented book available on French Jewry. Its author notes that Jews from Palestine arrived in Gaul (France) as early as 135 C.E., following the revolt by Bar Kokhba.

> The Christianization of the Roman Empire under Constantine the Great . . . and the restrictions that gradually came to be imposed on the Jews, favored their emigration, particularly to Gaul, which was slower to become Christianized . . . . The settlement of Jews along an axis following the valley of the Rhône and extending from that of the Saône to its juncture with the Rhine corresponds to the route taken by the Roman legions, which Jews followed as soldiers, tradesmen, or merchants in search of a better life and more favorable economic conditions (p. 4).

With the establishment of the Carolingian Empire under Pepin, French Jews were well treated and socially mobile. Especially in their own state of Narbonne, they enjoyed self-governance and moved into the highest political and economic advisory positions. Furthermore, Jews in France "lacking the Talmud, adhered closely to the text of the

Bible and to certain oral traditions. There existed a religious confusion between Judaism and Christianity, both with regard to prescriptions and to worship" (p. 5). We see such a synthesis of the two faiths in the Christian and Jewish icons of Calalus.

In addition to being the home of an autonomous Jewish state, one founded at exactly the same time as Calalus, France was also the birthplace of the Cabala. Out-of-place and anachronistic Masonic symbols have served as one of the strongest arguments in the attempt to discredit the Calalus Texts. We can trace them back to the same source as many other elements in this Frankish Jewish colony:

> Provence, land of philosophy, was also a land of mysticism. It is there that the *Sefer-ha-Bahir* (Book of Brightness), the first document of theosophic kabbalism, was compiled on the basis of oriental sources . . . . Abrah ben Isaac, president of the rabbinical court of Narbonne (d. 1180), and especially Isaac the Blind (1160?-1235) – grandson of Abraham ben Isaac...developed a contemplative mysticism. (Benbassa p. 34).

Returning to Los Lunas, we may ask if there are any Cabalistic markings around the Decalogue Stone? The answer is yes. High above the location is a mesa with the remains of a stone village; cisterns, roads, floorplans, and watchtowers are still evident. The boulders forming the edge of the dropoff contain numerous petroglyphs. The two illustrated here are unparalleled in the thousands of southwestern Indian rock carvings and paintings I have been able to examine, either in the field or in print.

Fig. 15. Torah, Merkabah and Sefirot petroglyph on Hidden Mountain.

Fig. 16. Star of David and Ten Commandments petroglyph on Hidden Mountain.

The petroglyph presented in Fig. 15 incorporates the Torah (Law of Moses) with the Heavenly Chariot (Merkabah) and Sefirot, or Tree of Illuminations. These devices first appeared in the Heikalot Books, central Cabalistic texts based in turn on the biblical Book of Ezekiel. Traveling from Babylon to France to Spain, the mystical traditions of the Cabala were not placed in writing until the twelfth century, but they were originated by the same Sephardic Jews as we suggest founded

96

Calalus. Note that the wheels of the chariot are drawn to incorporate the Pythagorean theorem; metaphorically, this taught that mathematical wisdom could raise mankind to a perfected state (Bernstein 1984 p. 132). An important teaching contained in the Tree of Illuminations is the perfectibility of the world through human endeavor, often expressed in Judaic tradition as Tikkun Olah – perfecting the universe.

In the second petroglyph (fig. 16) we see what seems to be an Indian migration symbol. But instead of a cross or swastika, common forms on such petroglyphs, we have a six-pronged star. The tribes whose migration map this is did not wander to the four directions, as so many of the Pueblo peoples and Hopi clans did. Also, the *paihas* or turning points actually end in forks, implying, again, a dispersal. Coming out of one of the rays, and designed in such a fashion as to suggest a clan symbol, is a geometric object that surely has no meaning in the Pueblo world. I count ten divisions on the two panels and believe that this petroglyph represents the Decalogue. If interpreted as other petroglyphs, it shows, in our opinion, the twelve tribes of Israel scattered from a central point with the priestly tribe of the Levites (Cohanim) entrusted with carrying the Ten Commandments.

Calalus was finally reconquered by the Toltecs. We do not know what revenge may have been taken on the Jewish settlers. Perhaps Hidden Mountain was their Massada, a last stand before they were wiped out. Perhaps Calalus women and some of the men were taken into surrounding Pueblo Indian groups, either as refugees or slaves. Years afterward, their descendents carved their story in petroglyphs, and many centuries afterward exiled Spanish Jews chose Los Quelites as their New Jerusalem.

No one has ever explained the meaning of the word Calalus. I believe it comes from Hebrew KLL לֹלכ with the Latin ending –us. The root means "deserted, empty." The meaning is thus Desertland.

In a whisper, our *chueta* concluded by saying that he believed there was a cave beneath the stone – perhaps the reason it now rests at an incline as though sunken on one side? At one time there had been an earthquake. In the cave was the Ark of the Covenant. There were those who wanted to build a new Temple of Jerusalem on Hidden Mountain. It was their duty as Levites and Cohanim, sextons and priests. Finally, it was his belief that the lettering of the Ten Commandments was engraved by the finger of God, "electrically." I prefer to date it to eighth-century Byzantine Hebrew, the sort of inscription as might be commissioned by Israel of Calalus.

Go, then, and see New Mexico's Decalogue Stone. If you are meant to find it, you will.

References and Suggestions for Further Reading

Eli Barnavi, ed., *A Historical Atlas of the Jewish People from the Time of the Patriarchs to the Present* (New York: Schocken, 1992).

Henrietta Bernstein, *Cabalah Primer: Introduction to the English/Hebrew Cabalah* (Marina del Rey, Calif.: Devorss, 1984).

Esther Benbassa,. *The Jews of France* (Princeton, N.J.: Princeton University Press, 1999).

David Biale, *Cultures of the Jews. A New History* (New York: Schocken, 2002).

Cyclone Covey, *Calalus: A Roman Jewish Colony in America from the Time of Charlemagne Through Alfred the Great* (Columbus, Ga.: ISAC Press, 2001); *The Yuchi/Yuki Nonplus* (Columbus, Ga.: Institute for the Study of American Cultures, 2002); *A Critical Reprise of 'Aboriginal' American History*, 4th ed. (Published by the Author, 2004).

David Allen Deal, *The Nexus. Spoken Language. The Link Between the Mayan and Semitic During Pre-Columbian Times* (Columbus, Ga.: ISAC Press, 1993).

ESOP=*Epigraphic Society Occasional Publications.* (1974-present).

Gloria Farley, *In Plain Sight. Old World Records in Ancient America* (Columbus, Ga.: ISAC Press, 1994).

Barry Fell, *America B.C.* Revised ed. (New York: Pocket Books, 1989).

Oswald White Bear Fredericks and Frank Waters, *Book of the Hopi* (New York: Viking Press, 1963)

David M. Gitlitz, *Secrecy and Deceit. The Religion of the Crypto-Jews* (Albuquerque: University of New Mexico Press, 2002).

Cyrus H. Gordon, *Before Columbus* (New York: Crown, 1971).

Elizabeth C. Hirschman. *Melungeons: The Last Lost Tribe in America* (Macon, Ga.: Mercer University Press, 2005).

Hans Jensen, *Sign, Symbol and Script. An Account of Man's Efforts to Write,* 3rd ed. (New York: Putnam, 1969).

N. Brent Kennedy, *The Melungeons: The Resurrection of a Proud People.* Revised ed. (Macon, Ga.: Mercer University Press, 1998).

Robert C. Mainfort and Mary L. Kwas, "The Bat Creek Stone Revisited: A Fraud Exposed," American Antiquity 64 (Oct. 2004) 761-769.

J. Houston McCulloch, "The Bat Creek Stone," website at http://www.econ.ohio-state.edu/jhm/arch/batcrk.html.

David McCutchen, *The Red Record. The Walam Olum: The Oldest Native North American History.* Garden City Park, N.Y.: Avery Publishing, 1993.

Thomas O. Mills, *The Truth* (Privately Published, 1998).

Steve Olson, *Mapping Human History. Discovering the Past Through Our Genes* (Boston: Houghton Mifflin, 2002).

Timothy R. Pauketat and Diana DiPaolo Loren, ed., *North American Archaeology* (Oxford: Blackwell, 2005).

William H. Prescott, *History of the Conquest of Mexico & History of the Conquest of Peru* (New York: Modern Library, 1975).

Constantine Samuel Rafinesque, *Ancient History, or Annals of Kentucky: with a Survey of the Ancient Monuments of North America, and a Tabular View of the Principal Languages and Primitive Nations of the Whole Earth* (Frankfort, Ky.: Printed for the author, 1824). Available online courtesy of the Filson Historical Society and University of Chicago Press at http://memory.loc.gov/.

Polly Schaafsma, *Indian Rock Art of the Southwest* (Albuquerque: University of New Mexico Press, 1980).

Dennis Tedlock, trans., *Popul Vuh. The Mayan Book of the Dawn of Life*. Revised ed. (New York: Touchstone, 1996).

Gunnar Thompson, *American Discovery. Our Multicultural Heritage* (Seattle, Wash.: Argonauts Misty Isles, 1994).

Arthur J. Zuckerman, *A Jewish Princedom in Feudal France, 768-900*. (New York: Columbia University Press, 1972).

THIS BOOK was set in the old-style serif typeface named for the French humanist printer Claude Garamond (*ca.* 1480 - 1561). A direct relationship between Garamond's letterforms and contemporary type can be found in the roman versions of the fonts Sabon, Granjon and Adobe Garamond.

Garamond came to prominence in the 1540s, first for a Greek typeface he was comissioned to create for the French king François I to be used in a series of texts by Robert Estienne. The French court later adopted Garamond's roman types for their printing and the typeface influenced type across France and Western Europe.

Garamond had likely seen Venetian old-style types from the printing shops of Aldus Manutius known for their editions of the Greek and Roman classical authors.

107

Made in the USA
Monee, IL
29 November 2019